Home Loans Not Rocket Science

Your First Time Home Buyers Guide:
For Texas Residents

Mario Galdos

ISBN-13: 978-0692446232 (Big Horn Media Moguls)

ISBN-10: 0692446230

DEDICATION

"It's an honor for me to not only be able to share some of the knowledge I've gained in the Mortgage Industry over the last decade and a half, but I'm also thrilled at the opportunity to be in a position to reach out and touch the lives of homebuyers all throughout the Lone Star State of Texas. I'm blessed beyond words to have a TEAM that helps me provide World Class superior service to the masses after enduring one of the most difficult market crashes the United States has ever suffered. What goes down, will always come back up; and I feel that we're at a point in time where this holds true for the present Real Estate Market and our Economy. We're definitely on the upward slope and I hope it stays this way for years to come.

I'm grateful to my wife Stephanie, my oldest son Darien, and my baby boy Triton for being supportive of my beliefs to make a difference in the lives of many who share the same American dream of home ownership. I love you.

I want to thank my good long time friend Marco Salinas with Credit 360 Consulting for approaching me with the idea of putting this book together. Marco is not only a true friend, but is also a Homebuyer who Triton Group had the honor of assisting when he purchased his home. Marco is also a business partner who I constantly refer to my clients when in need of special attention regarding their credit needs. Working with Marco on this book has added another pillar to the foundation of our working relationship which I don't take for granted in the least. Thank you Marco!

Last but not least, I want to thank you for taking the time to read this dedication and transcript that's been put together for you to further understand the home buying process. This book has been put together to help aid any confusion with the home buying process. We want to make this process as simple as possible for each and every potential home owner. We're grateful for the opportunity to serve you, and Triton Group firmly believes that you shouldn't settle for less when it comes to service. It's Home Loans. Not Rocket Science. "

TABLE OF CONTENTS

INTRODUCTION: Who is Mario Galdos?

Hello and welcome to today's program. My name is Marco Salinas and joining me is mortgage expert and Founder of Triton Group a subsidiary of Directions Equity Home Loan, Mario Galdos. Mario is going to share his years of experience in helping thousands of first time home buyers achieve the American dream of home ownership.

Just a little background about Mario: Mario is a Banking and Finance expert and is a Senior Residential Mortgage Loan

Originator. He has been in the mortgage industry since 2005, and in the banking and finance industry since the year 2000. After being one of the few lenders in Texas to weather the mortgage crisis of 2008, Mario adapted his business to the economic changes that took place and positioned himself as a reliable and honest lender. Now making a very strong name for himself in San Antonio's real estate and mortgage industry, Mario has gone on to start his own mortgage branch, Triton Group, which is subsidiary of Directions Equity Home Loan. He and his team offer a wide variety of mortgage lending products to suit the needs of their customers from first time buyers to real estate investors.

Today we are going to be discussing the basics of the home buying process, specifically for those who are doing this for the very first time. This is going to be presented through the lens and guidance of the mortgage lender. We're going to cover things such as down payment, credit score requirements, different loan programs that exist today, why you can save money in the long run by purchasing a home over renting, some of the basic buyer programs that are available to you which will assist you in purchasing your first home, and many other topics surrounding the first time home buying experience. Without putting this off any longer, let's dive in. Mario, welcome to the program.

Mario: Hello, how are you doing Marco?

Marco: I'm doing great. Thank you for joining us here today. I'm excited to talk a little bit more about you and your company, Triton Group, and to get a little bit of knowledge and background on your area of expertise, which is helping people to purchase homes, specifically their first home. This is not something that you started doing yesterday.

A few things I want to cover include who/what Triton Group is? What types of home buyers you can help? Is your focus only on first time home buyers? Can you help other people in the process?

Mario: Were definitely here to help the first time home buyer, but also pride ourselves on helping the recurring home buyer purchase their move up or investment home.

Triton Group is something that I founded towards the end of 2014, really in an effort to try to build and grow my team. I wanted to expand myself and not just my name. I got to the point where I got busier so I brought on an assistant to not only help me keep a steady process flow, put pride into the hard work we deliver, and keep home buying and obtaining a mortgage as simple and easy as possible. To ensure this happened I felt it was necessary to take the next step and officially brand a team. Working with Directions Equity since 2009 helped me understand the importance of constantly grooming and perfecting a machine. I'm proud to brand myself at a company that believes in maintaining a well oiled machine. So I made a home for my team Triton Group at Directions Equity Home Loan.

On a side note, what makes Triton Group even more exciting to me is the fact that it's named after my new born son, Triton, who was born in July 2014.

Marco: Awesome. I like how you came up with the name for your company and why you chose to do what you did in starting your own subsidiary of Directions Equity. Now I'd like to know a little bit more about you personally. As I mentioned earlier, you're not new to mortgages. My understanding, in fact, is that you've actually been around for a good while. As I mentioned,you've actually been in the Mortgage and Banking industry since the year 2000.

Why don't you tell us a little bit about how that all started for you. As well as what your motivation has been through the years since you started to bring yourself to not only where you are at this present moment here, but now you've actually got your own branch office and team. Where did you start, what were your humble beginnings in the mortgage industry? Tell us, has it been an easy road for you through the years? Some people reading this won't know, but the mortgage industry hasn't always been as great as it is, on the rise from when you started to where you are today. Can you elaborate a little bit for us as to where you got started, what your motivation is, as well as how you weathered some of those difficult storms through the industry?

Mario: Absolutely. In the year 2000 I had my first son Darien Alexander.

Becoming a father made me realize that I needed to try and put everything together, and position myself, my son and his mother in a way that created a future for us. I started working in the banking industry in the year 2000 from the bottom, up. Initially I was a teller in one of these little grocery store branch locations where I was cross trained in new accounts and a variety of other banking products. In my learning process It was mandatory to cross sell a variety of products, and be fearless when approaching people about investments, retirement accounts, and mortgages. One thing that really elevated me above other Associates was that I had the ability to talk to people and explain things in great detail. Enough to make them feel comfortable and go through an entire process with me.

I loved banking, but for anyone who doesn't know it's very under appreciated and I realized that I could personally make a difference in people's lives by providing them with service that is superior to that of most who did and still do mortgages today. I had talked about mortgages for years while working in banking and the timing was perfect. Everybody, and anybody could get qualified for a home. I dove right in and fit in perfectly. I'll always remember my first boss. I know I gave him a ton of grief with all the questions I asked, but he really put a lot of time and effort into coaching me correctly, and giving me the confidence to communicate with people about the home buying process.

As most know, 2007 began a down turn and fall in the mortgage market which ultimately led to the big crash in 2008. It was amazing how everything changed. It was like a switch, one day your able to help anyone regardless of how bad their credit and finances were, and the next day theres only a few select programs that were regulated. I recall having several difficult conversations about how I was no longer able to help a home buyer, or how the home they were refinancing didn't appraise for the value needed to make a deal work. It was really heart breaking.

In 2010, after having weathered a few years into the mortgage crash, I had a conversation with an account representative from a major bank. He told me that although the market had changed, what goes down, eventually comes back up and that If I just kept trucking along, things would work out and eventually I would have the opportunity to resume my dream of helping change the lives of others by helping them purchase their first home, second home, investment home or forever home. He went on to say that I would be at a higher level amongst other loan officers in the industry since I weathered a very difficult storm brought on by the crash. He was right. Here we are years later in one of the healthiest markets I've ever seen, and the demand for home ownership in Texas continues to rise. I'm truly blessed to be a part of this.

Marco: Correct me if I'm wrong, Mario, but I understand that you're fluent in Engish and Spanish, is that correct?

Mario: Yes sir. I owe it to my parents for teaching me Spanish at a young age and instilling it into my daily routine to make sure I didn't forget it. I'm very grateful for that. I think that being bilingual has really opened a lot of doors for me, especially being in Texas. I've really been able to reach a lot more people just because I am bilingual and fluent in both English and Spanish.

Marco: I understand that you're a new father for the second time. Tell us a little bit more about that and how your oldest son was big part of your motivation and influence in your early years.

Mario: My oldest son Darien Alexander has the rock that grounded me. After he was born he, his mother and I all three lived together in this little one bedroom apartment where, to be honest, he had his crib inside the walk in closet, which was conveniently sized well enough to be able to hold a crib and still hold our clothes - not that we had a lot of belongings at that time being so young. We basically started from scratch really just trying to build a life and solid foundation for Darien.

Luckily, because I developed great customer service skills quickly, I excelled quickly at the bank I was working for. I actually moved in to a supervisory position within 3 months, and within a year and a half I actually moved into the assistant manager position. I was there for a few years and was offered my final position as Branch Manager for one of the bank locations.

Those years had very challenging moments, and It had it's great moments. Just being in banking I had the ability to really lift my family up from being in that one bedroom to a two bedroom, to renting a house.

It was very important to me to plant all the essential seeds for Darien to have a stable life. I wanted to position myself well enough to where we weren't going to struggle. Although struggle and hard work makes you stronger it's not easy, but life isn't easy. I'm blessed to have had that experience since it ultimately taught me some great things and led me to where I am today.

Marco: Let's fast froward a couple years to the time period known as the "mortgage meltdown". What year did that take place, and tell me about your personal experience with the industry imploding on itself, so to speak, and what happened to the majority of loan officers that were around prior to this meltdown?

Mario: As mentioned, I started in the mortgage industry in 2005 where everyone with a pulse could basically get a home loan. I was given an opportunity to work at this retail mortgage company. It was set up as a call center where I would get a list of homebuyers who inquired about getting a home loan. I had to to call and convince them of why it was a good idea to do so. At the time I was originating loans in different states, offering programs that would allow people to tap into equity they didn't have and pay off credit cards that had accumulated balances on them.

These products were really creative and it was incredible that they gave people the opportunity who would have never bought or refinanced a home, the opportunity to not only purchase but cash out on equity with very sub par credit. As most know, this led to the disaster which I noticed first hand in the middle of 2007 and by the time 2008 was here I was witness to the fall of several major mortgage companies who were considered major players. It was incredible and devastating to watch.

As soon as I could tell that things were about to changing (2007) I went up from the retail office I was at to a brokerage because I started realizing that the products that I was able to give some of the clients were going away and several mortgage companies were closing their doors.

It was pretty unfortunate because I remember this Home Owner who was looking to refinance their home. We were within a few days of closing and all we needed for final approval was the appraisal. This deal was going to save the home owner thousands monthly since we were helping her consolidate some debt. She needed a certain value in order to refinance her home, and the home appraisal came in $40,000 short. I remember thinking to myself that there was a definitely a market change on the way. Unfortunately I was unable to help that homeowner finalize her refinance. It broke my heart because she was really looking forward to the overall benefit of reducing some of her debt load. I knew she had a very big need for this to happen and personally felt responsible as If I had taken that hope away. Within a few months I moved to the brokerage I mentioned earlier where I was able to work with some of the more traditional conforming products like Conventional, FHA, VA and USDA loans.

With that transition came a lot of hardship. I realized that although my boss was great and taught me confidence in myself, I was also taught shortcuts not only by him but by the system that had been created to qualify potential home buyers and existing home owners. I didn't know how to actually qualify a potential home buyer based off their accurate income that they were reflecting on their tax returns, W2's, pay stubs, bank statements, etc. These were things that were unbeknownst to me. It really took me back.

I've mentioned several times that I started my mortgage career in 2005, but it's almost like I started again in 2008 just because it was a brand new deal. Starting from scratch and adjusting to the programs that were available. It took me a little bit of time to be able to not only understand the concept of how these programs worked so that I could explain it correctly, but to really micro analyze the details of these programs like like I did when I was at the bank or when I first started in the mortgage industry. I wanted to become more of a teacher of the process. The process is something that I think is very valuable.

This is where I feel I create the most value for my home buyers today. PROCESS. Understanding Step 1 which is getting pre-approved/Pre-qualified is actually the most important step before even beginning to look for a home. It will help you set expectations about credit, what you qualify for, how much you qualify for and what steps you'll need to take to get the home. This all happens in the first conversation with anyone on my Team at Triton Group. Most importantly it will set the expectations for the entire process all the way to closing.

I had to figure out a way to help more home buyers or people who were looking to refinance. Really what I realized was that the market for refinances, which was something that I had built up so greatly, was almost pretty much gone. Rates had started to spike, products were going away, people who had ample opportunities to buy homes or refinance didn’t have those opportunities anymore, they just didn't exist.

It got to a point where I was telling 70% of people that I spoke to that I couldn’t help them. It was difficult to find the 30%. I had to start finding different outlets and different avenues to be able to accomplish helping clients achieve their home purchasing or home refinancing goals. Again, I learned as much as I possibly could. Basically started pounding the pavement to try to get my name out as much as I possibly could. Guiding homebuyers and giving them valuable information to assist them with re building their credit and how to manage their assets. I gathered a wealth of information about the products I could offer and became an expert on them. This was also challenging since it was a moving target because even the conforming programs I offered were being re-written and tightened up because of the market crash. There were a few times where I would offer a home buyer something one day and then not even a week later it would have a different set of rules. It was very difficult there for quite a while.

Unfortunately I saw a decline in the business. At the same time the one thing that kept me very motivated about the whole thing was the fact that I knew that at some point everything would settle down. That's what everybody always said, at some point things will bounce back. I weathered the storm and was able to continue to provide for my son Darien in the way that I felt was definitely going to be fruitful for him and for us as a little family.

Unfortunately his mother and I had divorced several years before that because being as young as we were it didn't work out for us, but we remained friends. In that transition Darien and I had purchased a home. We moved out to a little town called Schertz, Texas, which is exciting enough because that's where my office and home of Triton Group is at now.

I stayed with the brokerage I was at for a few years and felt it was time to venture to a company that had a vision to grow. I knew the broker for several years and switched my license to Direction Equity at the beginning of 2009. From there I did have an unfortunate incident happen where my son Darien's mom passed away. Unfortunately this created a hardship in my life since I had never lost somebody so close in age to myself, let alone so close to my little family. Not only for the loss of my sons mother, but really more so for the loss that my son felt with losing his mother. It was something that, again, was a little bit of a curve ball.

In 2010 I met the girl that was to become my wife years late, Stephanie Sommerlad. Having Stephanie come into mine and Darien's life was a very life changing event for us. We shared the same goals, and the same visions. Ultimately she became a mother to Darien. This was something that gave me peace of mind in order to continue moving forward with ultimately building and creating my team under

Directions Equity Home Loan, Triton Group.

Marco: Mario, that is a very, amazing personal testimony of your career and life experiences. As I mentioned at the beginning of this topic, your career hasn't just been this perfect straight arrow upward, you had many, many, many challenges and difficulties that you had to endure and overcome. All the while it seems that you really kept your mind focused on your goals and obligations. Those who had been entrusted to your care, such as your son, and now your new wife and your new son.

It's a very, very beautiful, actually, story that you shared with us. I really appreciate you filling us in on all of those personal life occurrences that you had because that's not always easy to talk about. I have a much better understanding of your passion in this industry and why you do what you do and why you're so motivated to help people to become first time home owners, because you also knew what it felt like to start off in that humble little apartment or that humble rental home.

Being able to transition into a better situation for yourself and for your family is really priceless. It's obvious in the story that you speak from experience.

I also want to ask you, through all those years and all of those struggles and all your growth and where you've become now, here today, as President of your own branch, Triton Group, is there any one in particular that had a personal impact on you as far as your motivation, your guidance in your career? Is there anyone that comes to your mind, that stands out to you that has really assisted you and really led you and showed you the way, so to speak, in this industry?

Mario: I really have to say that there were several people who influenced me and I can't just pin point one person. The first, keeping it really close to my family, is my mother. My mom is actively a real state agent and has been a real estate agent since the year 2000. Her influence and watching her grow and develop her business was something that inspired me, This ultimately is was what led me into the mortgage industry and kept me in the mortgage industry. She had unrelenting perseverance which was inspiring.

When that 2008 market crashed she weathered the storm at the same time I did. It was one of those things where I wanted to make my mom proud, I wanted to weather that storm with her, and continue to help make a difference in peoples lives day in and day out, which is something that she really put a lot of pride into. I think first and foremost I've got to give it to my mom for providing me that inspiration and the dedication that ultimately is some of that fueled the passion that I have now.

Secondly, I think it's funny enough my first branch manager, who was ultimately the first broker I worked with in the retail mortgage environment when I got into the business in 2005. He was my manager and again, my first broker; his name was Brien Lawler. He had so much patience for me. I'm like a sponge when it comes to learning things. It's one of those things where Brien understood that about me, but knew that I had to wrap my head completely around every single thing so that I could regurgitate it and ensure it as knowledge to other potential home buyers.

He mentored me. I think more so, he taught me how to be confident in myself with what I was trying to conveying to a client in their best interest. Home buying tends to be a very emotional thing for people. With that emotion there's almost a roller coaster that people go up and down in trying to grasp the concept of what they're doing. Then obviously assuming this endeavor of home buying can almost come off as being a little complicated and intimidating. That's something that Brien helped me with which helped me help more people. I took what he said and gave it back to people in my own words.

People who know me also know that I've been a musician for years. My music Producer and close friend Bryan Scott was also a huge influence. What made him really special was the fact that he taught me the importance of the details. The details, as simple as they sound, are really the most important things that you can put into anything that you do in life. If you're going to go after something and if you're going to chase something, to me it's very important that you're conveying every single thing as much as you possible can to that person that you're trying to help. You need to be able to make it easy for them to understand what you're trying to accomplish. I realized that I need to not only put more time into the details when playing in the band I was in, but this mindset would really change how i approached helping potential home buyers purchase their home in the future.

He helped me understand the importance of not only marketing myself in a way that was easy to understand, but also to have that same confidence that the other Brien taught me in myself to be able to follow my ideas, and my vision, and my dreams and make them a reality. That's something that he was very successful at doing himself, and gave him a lot of success in his musical career.

CHAPTER 1- Home Buyer Misconceptions

Marco: Mario, that is an absolutely incredible story that you just shared with us. I really appreciate you talking a little bit about those who influenced you, because we all have those that we've encountered in our lives that have really assisted us and given us that extra push or strength, so to speak, that we need. That really is a powerful message that you have there from those individuals that touched you in your life, both Brien, and Bryan and your mother. Of course moms are always a strong, strong influence and support system for us. It's a really beautiful thing.

You mentioned with some of this guidance that you received from those mentors, that these individuals really helped you to form the person that you have become today, which is someone that is really, really passionate and dedicated to helping individuals to became home owners. Let's transition back again a little bit more towards that topic.

I'm really curious, I hear a lot of things when I'm out there and I'm talking to people myself, personally, about the home buying process which is, it's something that's going to be extremely, extremely difficult, or "I don't even want to give it chance because I know there's not even any hope for me because of X, Y, Z." I'm just wanting to know from you, Mario, in all your years of experience, what is probably the most common misconception that you hear which is preventing the average first time buyer, so to speak, from actually going and achieving that dream of home ownership?

Mario: I think that the answer is actually quite simple. Really what it comes down to is that there's a misconception over how complicated the process is. When you over complicate something it tends to intimidate you to the point where you're scared of even trying it. That's something that I notice is the biggest obstacle that most first time home buyers have. Then even the recurring home buyer who's looking to upgrade their home whether it be their second home that they're going to live in for the next 20, 30 years, or whether it be their forever home, or their retirement home. Potential Homebuyers get intimidated with the process of purchasing and what needs to happen.

A lot of those fears come from social media and from the internet, which truly is a wealth of knowledge, but also has a lot of information that isn't accurate. I think that's one thing that I really try to push whenever I'm explaining things to people. I'm their "expert", I want them to rely on me 100% to help educate them in the best way possible. Ultimately this is what's going to make that home purchase a reality.

Another thing that makes home buyers apprehensive is credit, which is something that is very important to home buying and something that they need to consider important. Even with the potential home buyer who might think their credit isn't ready yet, they need to still try. I think just trying can take out some of that mystery, and worry over what the goal is, which is of course actually purchasing a home.

I do a full credit, income and asset analysis up front verifying not only what they say in the initial conversation had, but take the next steps to fully verify and review everything thoroughly to ensure they won't have any trouble in getting financing. This is a great value since most banks, and brokers don't do this. Triton Group at Directions Equity Home Loan is actually considered a Banker which is a hybrid of both Banks and Brokers. We have in house underwriting, processing, and closing like a bank would, but have the flexibility of selling the loan at closing to multiple investors who have different products available making it easier to help more home buyers.

This also helps the home buyer who's self-employed understand exactly how much they qualify for, or the commission only home buyer. By fully understanding their tax returns, and how they get paid I can paint the right picture for my underwriter to ensure the loan gets approved without any issues. For me, it's all about trying to position them to be able to help them accomplish their goal. People tend to over complicate and worry about the fact that they might not be able to get into the home because of their income, because of their credit, maybe they don't have the money to put down, but that's what I'm here for; I'm here to take that element away.

When it comes to the credit, not everybody has paid everything on time. The reality behind people actually paying their bills on time and actually getting themselves into, or having credit issues is really more common than I think most people think it is. Although it's something that will need to be worked on, I've personally assisted home buyers with credit over the years to not only learn the basics and the fundamentals of how credit works, but I've also positioned myself with a great team that will help me, help these potential home buyers become actual home buyers within a realistic time frame.

I've also been fortunate enough to work side by side with a credit repair agency nnamed Credit 360 Consulting. Credit 360 Consulting company has helped not only a a great deal of clients that came to me with some credit issues, but have helped my personal friends and then some extended family as well which ultimately helped them purchase a home. For me to give a personal recommendation and referral to my family is huge, because I'm endorsing someone and I don't take that lightly. I can tell you that Credit 360

Consulting is definitely the place that I like to refer the majority of my credit challenged clients who need a little bit of extra attention with their credit.

Marco: It sounds to me that what your saying is that individuals that might have potential credit challenges should not let that be the reason why they hold themselves back, so to speak, from actually picking up the phone and calling you guys just to find out where they stand. It sounds like you've got options, either to help them there in-house with some of your own guidance, or worse case scenario if there's extensive work that needs to be done you obviously do have resources that you can refer them out to. It sounds like you have that whole area covered and your prospective clients should never, ever let credit be the reason why they tell themselves that there's no chance for to purchase a home. Do you agree?

Mario: That's absolutely right, and is exactly what I'm tying to say. Credit, as important as it is to the process of purchasing a home shouldn't be the sole focus of why somebody thinks that they can't even try. I think that you have to try to be able to know what needs to happen. In todays market I every five out of ten people that approach me and tell me that they have concerns about their credit end up qualifying. Had they not tried they would never have known that. I want to help potential home buyers and become their expert. I want to teach them what needs to happen in order to be able to accomplish their home purchasing goals.

Marco: That's incredible. In addition to credit, another one of those hot topic items is a lot of times the topic of down payment. A lot of people feel that "oh, my family member told me that I was going to need to put down 20% to be able to purchase a home, and to be quite honest I don't think that I'll ever have 20% of the money that I'll need to purchase this home." What are the realistic expectations for down payments?

Because that is another item that really hinders a lot of people from taking steps to even just remotely look into their home buying process. Can you clear the air on that just a little bit?

Mario: Yeah. There's definitely a wide variety of products that are available in today's market. One of them being for the first time home buyer we have programs that offer very little to no money down. We'll start with the USDA loan, which is the loan type that offers 100% financing. Right off the bat there is a home product that allows for 100% financing, meaning no money down. Really even just a small deposit of $500 just to get themselves into the home. Those products are available and it is something that's out there and very commonly used.

There's also products like the VA loan, which applies to veterans, that offers 100% financing as well. That's something that whenever I get the phone call from a veteran I get excited because I love helping our military, but really more so I love the fact that I can put them into something without having to worry about having any money down. Plus VA offers lot of perks like no Mortgage insurance which all other loan types require to have if you're not putting 20% down. Mortgage insurance is an insurance that is charged by the lender when putting less than 20% down to protect the lender against losses due to foreclosure.

Even for the person that's not military, we offer products with as little as 3% down. The 3% down product is going to be geared towards first time home buyers, so that is a dedicated first time home buyer product. It's great because it's going to offer you the same conveniences that somebody who's putting the 5-10% down have as well. Meaning your your payments going to reduce because this mortgage insurance will automatically drop off. It's something that's great because it really helps keep the home buyer motivated to make the payments up until the point where ultimately they're going to have enough equity to not have to pay this additional insurance, which is great.

There's another product which is the FHA product, again that offers 3.5% financing. The FHA product is great because it really can help clients who are either in that point who need a little bit of extra attention to things such as their debt to income ratio, which is numbers that I calculate basically for income versus how much you spend monthly. These are all things that I usually go over in great extent in our face to face meetings whenever we actually sit down to do the loan application together. It's really a great thing. There's definitely a wide variety of products out there that offer very little, to no money down. That should never be something that intimidates anybody from even just trying.

CHAPTER 2- Which Home Loan Program is Right for Me?

Marco: That's great information, Mario. I think that really clears a lot of things up, just those two topics alone, the down payment and the credit situation. Then of course you even elaborated a little bit on some of the programs that are out there. Are there any programs that you yourself, personally, are associated with or tied to that you can just put out there as an example? Especially being the fact that we're here in Texas, specifically San Antonio, which is known as Military city, USA. Do you have anything that maybe would appeal to a buyers program that might appeal to military or veterans and that sort of thing?

Mario: Definitely. This is something that I put a lot of pride into since I'm not helping not only our military service members, but really I like helping people in general. One thing that is unique to what I do is that I work with the Homes for Heroes program. The Homes for Heroes program as a program that was founded after 9/11 and the tragic incidents that happened. It was really put together in an effort to help all Active Duty Military, All Veterans, Doctors, Nurses, Teachers, Firefighters, and

Police Officers. What makes that exciting is that it really opens up the spectrum to try to help give back to the community.

I offer an incentive at closing to those in these professions which helps reduce the amount of closing costs they pay and reduces their bottom line at closing. It’s really exciting to be a part of this program. I can say that it's something that's very unique to myself, as a lender, because not a lot of lenders participate in this program. I know very few that are even in Texas that do this program, so I'm very proud to be able to offer that program, for again, not only the Active Duty Service Members, but for the Veterans, the Teachers, the Firefighters, Police Officers, Doctors, and Nurses.

Marco: That is really awesome, Mario. That is such a really amazing program to be associated with. I'm so happy to hear that they include so many others. Of course we already know that we consider our military “heroes”, but at the same time there's also a lot of other hard working heroes

CHAPTER 3- Making the American Dream A Reality/Closing Statement

Marco: That's pretty awesome. With that said Mario, do you have any personal stories, or are there any clients that might come to your mind that you may have recently helped out and maybe when they first came to you they were a little uncomfortable, or a little apprehensive, or just flat out maybe didn't even think they could get approved, or something to that effect that you can just share a story of someone that you helped obviously from going from that and ended up putting them in the home of their dreams?

Mario: Yeah, absolutely. Although I've helped several clients and several clients who've been nervous about the process, there is one friend of mine actually that I've known for some years that finally realized how hot the market is and decided to make the move to try to purchase a home. One of the first things that my friend asked me was what we needed to do. I told him basically from the get go that we needed to get an application going, at least to get a qualification going better yet, which was going to go over the overall home purchasing process. This is where I set expectations for what's going to happen during the process.

In the beginning it's really just information gathering. Gathering their name, their date of birth, their social, and income, and employment, and money in the bank. Just the small little details that are really going to help me put together an overall picture for them. Once I did that we actually set up a face to face meeting to discuss a little further detail exactly what was going to need to happen throughout the process. Because my client was a little more nervous, we definitely walked him through every single step with a fine tooth comb.

My client here, had a pretty interesting scenario because he wasn’t only self-employed but also had a spouse who was a teacher. This created a a mixed income situation. It's not uncommon to have mixed income situations when you have a married couple but this made him nervous since he didn't know if that would cause any problems with qualifying. We walked through the process step by step and I educated him with how I calculated the income for that business that he was running, and really broke it down to the final amount which helped give a bottom line number to really figure out and pin down exactly how much house they could qualify for. This really put him at ease and made him confident with the home purchase he ended up making. It was great because from being a complete novice to getting through the actual loan process, I really helped give him gain understanding, and education. After closing he was what I consider a “Raving Fan” about the home purchase process and ultimately this led him to refer me some of his own friends. Which I helped achieve home ownership by using the same service and process that I provided him.

A key element with his home purchase was that we ensured that he was able to qualify for that home up front. This kept there from being any stress while actually being in contract. I think something that's missed commonly in our industry, is not doing all the upfront work to make sure that the person qualifies. We did that. Once we got the loan into underwriting it was actually a pretty smooth process. This led to getting some of those family and friend referrals that he gave us.

Marco: That is awesome, Mario. Those are the kinds of stories and examples that I think people need to be aware of and hear so that they can also be reminded that they're not alone, there are a lot of others that have those feelings of, "Well this is just not going to work, and it's going to be too difficult, and there's really not anybody out there that can really help me." You've proven that this isn't the case for everyone.

This is great for anyone out there who is considering purchasing their first home, especially those that are currently in that rental situation. When you become a home owner you're actually putting money into something that you yourself own, that really is truly the American dream. There's really no other way to say that.

Mario: I love it. I love being able to help potential home buyers achieve the American Dream of Home Ownership over and over again. I think that's the thing that keeps me motivated and is very gratifying. It's very rewarding and ultimately you're helping somebody accomplish their dreams and obtain something that they can call theirs, that's actually their place to live in.

Marco: Mario, it's very, very clear now at this point in time that you are extremely dedicated to what you do. You've been around for a long time and it certainly doesn't sound like you're going anywhere else. In many cases with your new venture here at Triton Group it sounds like you're really just getting started. I think the sky's the limit for you and for all your clients that you guys are going to be assisting here over the years. I think that's a really, really exciting thing that you're able to do for people and that you're able to offer. I think you're in real privileged position to be able to assist people the way that you do. Quite frankly, I would imagine you probably sleep really good at night knowing that you're able to help people on a daily basis to really achieve these dreams that are so important, so truly important.

My final question to you now as we reach the end is, how can the potential first time home buyer find out more information about how to go about financing their home? How can they contact you, how can they reach you? What would you advise them to do as the first step if they're reading this right now, and how do they begin that process?

Mario: Just to keep it very simple, I think just trying to reach out to us and communicate is going the first thing. I'm going to make that every easy for the potential home buyer. Right off the bat I'm going to give you my website, because I think the website that I've built has all the details that I've mentioned that are extremely important to me in explaining a process. That website is: TritonGroupHomeLoans.com. I've made it so easy to not only navigate through the beginning of the loan process, but I've also put a custom made calculator which will let you calculate your payment for any price, any down payment, and it'll give you an accurate number with all the taxes and insurance. That way you can feel comfortable whenever you're ready to make that home purchase.

Marco: That calculator is located on the home page of your website?

Mario: Absolutely. It's located on the home page, and you can definitely get back to it just by clicking the "loan calculator" button at the very top of the header on the website there. Additionally, I've made some videos that really break down different parts of the process, and also break down the products, which is ultimately what I want to focus on. The process is very easy from start to finish. I will prove that to you within the first consultation. You can see that on the home page of my home page as well. I listed it in four steps. It's not quite three, but I feel that we can knock it out in four. I think that once you check it out you'll understand why once you check it out.

Additionally, the website also allows you the opportunity to apply online. That's something that can be found on all tabs of the website, on the header of all pages on the site, and additionally on the home page. You the opportunity to apply online and have the application come directly to me. If you're busy, which most of us are, this is going to give you that opportunity to do it from the convenience of your home late at night, while you're maybe on break at work, whatever your time is convenient for you.

I pride myself on quick service, and usually can get back to a client within the same business day after an application is filled out online. Even if you reach out over the phone. I pride myself on being available same day. I think prompt Follow up is something key in the loan industry that tends to be a very big problem for some clients that I've worked with who have started at other financial mortgage institutions. They've told me that they've gone through different places and that they don't get the attention that they've felt like they needed. That's something that I make sure I do the opposite of. I want to give you all the attention that you need to be able to make the best decision for you and your family, that ultimately is going to help you achieve your home purchase goal.

Marco: Absolutely. That's really helpful info there, Mario. It sounds like that calculator is something that someone who's just beginning the process of considering home ownership really needs to go and plug in that information to compare the cost of where they're at right now as renter versus becoming a home owner. Again, really weighing those pros to becoming a home owner and why it's so worth it, and so worthwhile to change that situation. What about a phone number, Mario? What's the best phone number to reach you and your staff right now?

Mario: Sure, I'm going to give you couple numbers, just because I like giving options to make it easy to get ahold of me or anyone on my team. My office line where you can reach either myself or my assistant is literally just one phone call away. That number is: 210-476-5523. You can also reach me on my personal cell at: 210-846-4725. I give out my personal cell number just in the event that if you need something right away I want you to be able to achieve that as quickly as possible.

Marco: Absolutely, Mario, I really want to thank you again for your time and most of all for sharing this wealth of information with those who will read this book and transcript of our conversation. I know it's going to be a real help for those who are interested in buying their home, or even for that matter for those who already have bought one but want to take things to the next step, whatever that might be in their personal lives.

Again, thank you so much for spending some time with us here today and for educating us and for the potential first time buyer who's tuning in. I hope that those that are reading will take action and will actually move forward in calling Mario or visiting his website. We really, really look forward to hearing about more success stories for those that encounter Mario and his really high level of work ethic and passion for his clients. Thank you again so much, Mario.

Mario: Thank you, Marco.